RT Chiwuta has always been intrigued by life's deeper questions and its inherent meaning. In his pursuit of understanding, he turned to writing and published his first book, *The Dichotic Dilemma*, with the hope of making the world a better place through his words. His new title, *Ottilie Rose, A Collection of Poems* is a continuation of that journey. He hopes his words can touch, move and inspire.

This book is dedicated to my parents, Reward and Ruth, who define what being a parent is with the sort of love and dedication that's humbling, informing, and ultimately enlightening. To my children, who came from my own flesh through the miracle of creation, a window into the unknown, my reason to be through the hardest of times. This book is also dedicated to Ronald and Ena Harper, whom I met through my marriage, and whose love for each other is what all the truest love tales are written about. However, it was their love for me, an African immigrant to the United Kingdom, and them, older white folk from a little village in Newcastle, which showed and inspired me to be present to looking beyond the racial barrier. Ultimately, the many human barriers.

RT Chiwuta

OTTILIE ROSE, A COLLECTION OF POEMS

An Observation and
Appreciation of Life

AUSTIN MACAULEY PUBLISHERS
LONDON * CAMBRIDGE * NEW YORK * SHARJAH

Copyright © RT Chiwuta 2025

The right of RT Chiwuta to be identified as author of this work has been asserted by the author in accordance with sections 77 and 78 of the Copyright, Designs and Patents Act 1988.

All rights reserved. No part of this publication may be reproduced, stored in a retrieval system, or transmitted in any form or by any means, electronic, mechanical, photocopying, recording, or otherwise, without the prior permission of the publishers.

Any person who commits any unauthorised act in relation to this publication may be liable to criminal prosecution and civil claims for damages.

A CIP catalogue record for this title is available from the British Library.

ISBN 9781398485075 (Paperback)
ISBN 9781398485181 (ePub e-book)

www.austinmacauley.com

First Published 2025
Austin Macauley Publishers Ltd®
1 Canada Square
Canary Wharf
London
E14 5AA

20250130

Introduction

Thank you for reading my book. As a way of introduction, I will explain a few things. This book is exclusively a book of poetry unlike *The Dichotic Dilemma,* my original foray into the world of writing where I explained and dissected my poetry. In this book, I will leave that to you. However, just like *The Dichotic Dilemma*, in this book, the poems are in the order in which I received them. I will, however, only give an introduction to one poem, the first one as its very personal.

Hence, this book and first poem are dedicated to and titled after my daughter, Ottilie Rose who was born at a time when I was coming out of a long, deep and very dark depression. She was like the sun, beaming into the darkness after the clouds of a terrible and violent storm are wasting away and it was written on her first birthday. So, it is the first poem of the book, and it is for my beautiful daughter.

However, this book is also dedicated to my son, my parents, humanity but most importantly to Ronald and Ena Harper who I met through my marriage. They deepened my understanding and appreciation of the human condition. How a young black man, raised in Africa, Zimbabwe and for all intents and purposes lived completely separately from white people there because of the politics and history of the country could come and have such a profound and loving relationship with two older white people from a little village in England. A perspective shifting and edifying experience.

The instant connection and love between the Harpers and I was so profound that they both said they wished that we had met earlier in their life so that they would have had more time to spend with me, more time to spend together. Proving to me as a consequence, that racism and hatred are not inherent human qualities. They are unfortunately in most cases if not all cases taught. Most importantly though, proving that love is transcendent and all conquering and that the solidarity of all of humankind is at least a possibility.

Mrs Harper, Ena Harper. I especially dedicate this book of poetry to her because she was my original, number one and biggest fan. I had and have a close relationship with both the Harpers but I had and have an especially close relationship with her. Our relationship was so natural.

As I said, she was my original fan, reading my book *The Dichotic Dilemma* numerous times and helping me to believe in myself and the book at a time when I really did not. However, most moving and pertinent to this book is that when I told her I was writing a new book, this book, she told me she really wanted to read it. She was ninety-two at the time so when she asked how long it would take me and I said I thought at least two years to compile the amount of poetry I needed, she told me to hurry up because she wanted to read it before she died. So, with all my heart, it is to her that I especially dedicate this poetry book to Ena Harper and I hope I complete it whilst you are still on this side of the gateway.

In closing, a special dedication to my parents for being my place of refuge in my darkest hour.

So, without further ado…

My Beautiful Ottilie Rose

When your mum searched and searched for your name,
With the love and passion, she always shows,
When she said Ottilie,
I wasn't sure,
Then others said it rhymes with otter,
What silly plonkers,
Jokes aside,
I truly know now,
That Ottilie doesn't rhyme with otter,
More like beauty or cutie.

They say there are known knowns,
And unknown unknowns,
You don't know what you don't know,
And when you think you know,
You don't know,
I thought I knew that I wanted a boy,
I didn't know if I wanted a girl.

But your mum knew,
That I didn't know,
How much I would love to be a father to a beautiful baby girl.

I went for a walk Ottilie,
For quite a while,
Through the wilderness of life,
In dark, dark forests,
Full of fierce fanged beasts,
Not knowing if I could or would make it through,
Not knowing if I would make it out,
But eventually I saw a glimmer,
A slight slither of light,
A golden ray of light,
Piercing through the darkness like a great deliverer,
And I knew then that I would make it through,
Make it out.

And as I came out into the sunshine,
Back to everything I knew,
You were now there too,
My precious little sunshine,
Just in time and on time,
To warm my heart.

The way you laugh and play,
And look right into my heart,
With your big brown eyes,
And blink,
Knowingly,
Like you know you came from me,
And blink and smile,
And blink and chuckle.

Ottie,
My little cutie,
Our little cutie,
Your first year in the world,
And I know your mother has loved you tenderly,
And I have loved you wholly,
And your older brother has loved you joyously.

Happy birthday,
And may your days be as long as time itself,
And your time be as joyous as the heavens will allow,
And as much as is within my powers,
I will see to it,
My poem on your first birthday my precious angel,
I love you so much,
My beautiful Ottilie Rose.

It's All Beautiful

The sun rise and the sunset,
Staring at the horizon on a beautiful shoreline,
Of course, yes, that's beautiful,
A beautiful starlit night,
The beaming full moon on a pitch-black night,
Love,
Romance,
Companionship,
Closeness,
A shared laugh with a dear friend,
The mountains,
And the verdant forests,
All beautiful.

But so is death,
Yes, death is beautiful too,
Suffering,
Pain and loss,
War,
Human strife,
Human suffering,
All suffering,
It's all beautiful,
To God's eye and in God's mind it's all beautiful.

For years and years my soul ached,
My head spun,
Trying to know,
Trying to understand,
Why there was so much suffering,
And what kind of God would allow it,
Even more so,
Create a world for it to occur in.

But today I know,
I truly know,
That truly, truly,
It's all beautiful.

The Purpose

What is the purpose?
Long I pondered,
With a heavy heart and aching soul,
A troubled mind and a troubled disposition.

To places I had to travel,
Beyond the mind's eye,
A life's quest,
A life's mission,
What is the purpose?
The purpose of everything,
The purpose of life,
The good and the bad,
The light and the dark,
The pain,
The misery,
The joy,
The laughter.

But, ultimately,
What is the purpose?
Why build this plain?
This plain of existence,
Yet the answer I found,

Clear as day,
That the purpose,
The purpose of it all is to be.

Only for the briefest moment,
Relative to the vast unending expanse of time,
A chance we have,
An opportunity we are granted,
An opportunity to be.

Indeed,
That's life's golden opportunity,
An opportunity to be,
Anything you choose to be,
So be.

Love is the Binding Fabric of the Human Condition

And hate its twin sibling,
Siblings locked in an eternal battle and dance,
This is life,
The Dichotic dilemma,
And we the pendulum,
Swinging between these two poles of love and hate,
This is life.

However,
In the end,
Love conquers all,
It is the ray of light piercing into the dark shadows of hate,
It is the thing that illuminates all,
It is the binding fabric of the human condition,
It is in the end the answer to all life's questions,
It is the thing that gives all meaning,
It is hope in the darkest times,
It is the realisation of pure ecstasy,
It is the experience of God on earth,
It is what we hope for,
It is what we dream of,
It is what we fight for,
Love is indeed the binding fabric of the human condition.
So, love.

Falling in Love

That cosmic miracle,
Once a stranger,
Now means the world,
One of life's true pleasures,
One of life's true miracles,
What could be more exciting?

That first eye contact,
That initial frisson of excitement,
How every day,
You meet so many people,
Yet this one,
A chemistry ignites from within,
An attraction you cannot help,
An attraction that's beyond your control,
A primal drive,
A transcendent attachment,
A cosmic miracle.

If only everyday felt like falling in love,
How wonderful life would be,
How magical.

Oh, to fall in love,
What a cosmic miracle,
Two insignificant interstellar dust particles,
Brought together by chance and happenstance,
Perchance to stay together till the end,
Bound by a moment in time,
For it all to happen,
What a cosmic miracle.

Death

The great beyond,
The other side of the locked door,
The great dichotomy,
For upon death, you find peace from life's tribulations,
You are set free from the torment of life.

Yet, the thought of death is one of life's greatest fears,
The event of it, an occasion of true pain and tragedy,
It is the great mystery.

What lies beyond the eternal sleep?
Is it just the end?
Or is it the beginning?
Perhaps the point we get the answer to all of life's questions.

How can a thing that was animate and warm a moment ago,
Be stiff, cold and inanimate just a moment later?
The last breath as though a force has left,
The spirit of life exited from the body,
What a mystery indeed.

Yet we all must and will get there,
It is the undeniable and uniting truth of life,
It is the thing that binds us all.

Perhaps it even is our greatest teacher,
Teaching us that in the end we are all one,
We come from the same place,
We return to the same place,
We are all united,
For we are all truly united in the inevitable fact of death.

So, what is life?
Well, it seems life is an opportunity to express the best of yourself,
The good in you,
For that seems the only meaningful choice,
For what is true is that we all live,
Yet we all must and surely will die,
And in death,
We are all truly united.

Life

What is life?
Life,
For a long time,
Seemingly forever,
I cursed you,
I hated you,
You seemed so cruel to me,
Cold and heartless,
Empty and meaningless,
Miserable,
Pointless.

Life,
I didn't know you then,
Yet I know you now.

So, what is life?
Life is an opportunity to look your son in the eye,
Look him in the eye and tell him you love him,
Then see the joy it brings,
This creature who just a short while ago didn't exist,
Yet now runs, laughs and smiles with careless abandon,
Made from your own flesh,

An opportunity to look at your daughter,
And marvel at how beautiful she is.

An opportunity to feel the love of your brothers and sisters,
Your loved ones,
Feel it course through your body,
Your soul,
Your entity,
Feel it engulf you in its warmth.

An opportunity to see the sunrise,
There at the horizon,
Oh, how amazing,
An opportunity to know God,
And meet God,
And God is the majestic wonder and beauty of the universe,
Yes, that is God,
That is Godly,
And life is an opportunity to be with all of that,
At its best,
That is what life should be,
And yes, that is what it is,
The pain and the beauty,
For how can you know beauty if you don't know pain.

Pain

I know you,
It seems you are always there,
And when you are not,
You are not too far away,
What are you for pain?

And yet it seems if I listen to you,
If I flow with you,
If I let you course through me,
Follow your path as you induce grief and suffering,
Follow you as you undulate and course through my consciousness,
At the end of the journey,
A mysterious alchemy seems to occur,
I seem to learn something from you, pain.

It seems there is a lesson,
A strange metaphysical alchemy,
Some kind of universal chemistry,
Some kind of transcendent teacher.

Are you a teacher, pain?
For it seems at the end of your lesson,
The sun shines even brighter,

Hence,
Maybe the collective pain of the human body will lead to a brighter sun,
On this celestial rock we call home,
A brighter day,
For much pain lives here.

Star

There you are,
Like a heavenly spot in the sky,
Seemingly harmless, adorable and meek,
Yet they say you are a blazing and raging ball of fire,
Yet you seem so beautiful and mild from where I see you,
Twinkly and peaceful.

Yet it seems that is the way of the universe,
The beauty and the beast side by side,
Like a moth to the flame,
Like a python to its prey,
Lured by the shimmering and glittering beautiful scales,
Only to be caught in an instant in the ferocious jaws,
Gripped by the unforgiving fangs,
To be squeezed and crushed to death,
Each struggle for breath,
Only assures death,
As the serpent squeezes tighter,
Till life is gone, squeezed from the unfortunate prey.

Star,
It seems you tell the story of life in your being,
The illusory veil of reality.

Star,
You look so beautiful,
Glistening and glittering in the dark,
Yet if I was to touch you,
All that would be left of me is a trail of vapour.

Life you trickster,
Star,
What stories you could tell,
They say you live for billions of years,
Oh, what stories you could tell,
Life,
You are so wondrous.

Sun

The ferocious disc of blazing glory,
The bringer of life,
The bringer of light,
There is no life without you.

No wonder the ancients worshipped you,
To them, your majesty was clear to see,
In the so-called Goldilocks zone, we are,
Just a bit further away and we would be too far from you,
Just a little bit closer and you would burn us to a cinder,
All this to be coincidence seems ever more unlikely,
The questions of life,
The answers will we ever find?

Sun,
When you come out, we rejoice and bask in your warmth,
When you are behind the clouds we miss you,
We need you for our health,
We need you for our sustenance,
Symbiotically and existentially attached we are to you,
When you come out, festivities abound,
The seaside suffers an invasion.

What glory,
We love you, sun,
Long may your rays descend from on high,
From so far in the distant universe,
So, life can flourish,
Find its course,
On this planet we call home,
Us complex yet simple earthlings.

Moon

You bright big disc in the sky,
Our nearest neighbour,
Our closest celestial friend,
What a sight you are to behold.

To see you suspended there in the dark sky,
What amazement you bring,
You come out when the sun goes in,
To partially illuminate the night sky.

We have visited you,
Man has stepped on your cold white sands,
They say you control the tides,
And some say strange things happen when you are full,
Perhaps they do,
The wondrous mysteries of the universe.

When I look at you,
I know there must be more out there,
It cannot be just us here,
And this cannot be all there is,
Thank you for inspiring mystery and wonder,
You beautiful disc in the night sky.

Woman

Wow,
I stand in awe at how amazing you are,
The great care giver,
The great comforter.

You nurse us with your very bosoms,
Your body a wonder and marvel,
The universe was truly inspired when you were created,
From your very body we emerge into this mortal plain,
Each and every one of us.

You are the great bringer of life,
The miracle of creation lives in you,
The very fate of our life on this living surface depends on you,
How at the miraculous point of conception a seed is planted within you,
And you nourish it,
And it grows within your very being.

Oh, what wonder,
Strong, resilient and steadfast you are,
Mother,
The great mother,
Mother to all, you are,

On a shrine we should put you,
So, we can marvel and spectate at your beauty,
Not just the physical,
Which can delude,
But the ethereal,
The true that is within and beyond,
The transcendent.

The one that will awaken in humanity,
The true discovery,
Of what it is to be a woman,
A blessing to us all,
The heavens were truly inspired when they conceived you,
Woman.

Father

Strong and ever present,
With a gentle firm hand, you guide the way,
Navigating me past life's trials and tribulations,
Stalwart you are,
A firm wall for me to lean on,
Tender and masculine.

From you I emerged,
And you have loved me as such,
A privilege and an honour to be your child,
Through confusion, chaos and pain,
On you I can depend,
On you I have depended.

May the heavens bless you,
As you have blessed me,
Long may you live,
Till it's time to rest,
And may your resting place,
Be heaven itself,
To all the loving fathers.

Israel, Palestine

Will you ever see peace?
Will you ever know peace?
The complexity of the human condition in full display,
When will you see,
That we are all human beings,
When the dust settles,
That's all we are,
Maybe one day.

Africa

African,
Rise,
This is your century,
The African renaissance,
They once said you were a continent with no history,
That is certainly not true,
All people have a history,
All people have a story to tell.

The dark continent they said,
Yet now you must rise into the light,
Europe rose,
Asia rises,
The Arab lands rise,
So now must you.

Africa,
African,
Much pain you have endured,
Seen fit to be exploited you were,
Yet now you must and should rise.

African leader,
Prioritise your people,
Work to leave a legacy,
A legacy such that you are remembered,
Remembered for how you raised your people.

May Africa be set free from those who might exploit her,
It's enough now,
That time has passed,
The shanty towns must go,
All the shanty towns of the world must go,
Let people live with dignity and pride,
Not like infested rats,
Breeding grounds for crime and discontent,
Surely, humanity can do better,
Surely, we can do more.

Africa,
African,
Rise,
Claim your rightful place at the table,
Show what you truly can be,
The African renaissance,
May the black skin that symbolises and marks the African,
Not be seen as a mark of inferiority anymore,
Time to end that paradigm,
Time to rewrite that matrix,
Time to retell that story,
Time to finally close that chapter.

Less than human it was said,
Ugly and worthless,
Fit for cages and to be caged,
The African.

May we not go into the next century,
Still living the consequences of that mindset,
May we in this time witness the African resurgence,
African, you are not intellectually inferior as some try to prove,
So, they can keep you in a place of inferiority and subservience.

It's time to set yourself free,
Just as the European found his prosperity by conquering and taking fate into his own hands,
Now you too must take your fate into your own hands,
Let go of the inferiority complex,
You are more than worthy,
Unite,
Love your neighbour,
Stand as one.

African leader,
It is to you I speak,
Raise your people,
The European conqueror raised his people,
Now so must you.
Africa,
African,
Rise.

Universe

Incredible and endless,
At a scale beyond human comprehension,
They say it all started in a big bang,
All in an instant,
Yet the mind wonders,
What came before the big bang?
In what space did the big bang occur?
The founding constituent particles of the big bang,
Where did they come from?

To dispute the scientists seems folly,
As science has achieved so much,
Science understands so much,
Science has done so much,
Yet science only entails what the human eye can see,
What the human mind can conceive.

So, what lies beyond human sight?
What lies beyond the human mind?
What lies beyond human understanding?

What of superposition?
What of quantum entanglement?
What of Schrodinger and his cat?

A glimpse into the wondrous unknown.
Universe,
I don't believe you are just cold dead space with floating rocks and gas,
I believe you are alive,
I believe you are sentient,
Not in a way we can understand,
But in a way that's beyond our comprehension.

Just as to an ant I am a titan comprehending a world it could never comprehend,
And to the smallest particles in my body, I am a whole world,
A whole universe,
We are to you what they are to us.

Under the most powerful microscope,
All we are too is, seemingly dead space,
Yet we live, breathe and think,
And I say, so do you too,
Only in your own way,
In a grander way,
At a grander scale.

Us, mirrors of you,
Made in your image,
Smaller, lesser copies.

Made in your image we are as the scriptures say,
Very true it seems,
Excellently true.

The Miracle of Life

Our very existence,
A phenomenon of unbelievable magnitude,
That to really sit and ponder it,
Boggles the mind,
How are we even here?
Yet we take it all so for granted,
In our everyday existence,
Caught up in the process of being alive,
Being human,
Life's challenges and mundanity.

Yet to take a moment and truly reflect,
To look at your hand,
And observe the digits projecting from it,
To observe the front and the back of it,
Your fingernails,
Your fingerprints,
Each unique and individual,
Proving how special each life is,
Given its own unique signature,
The universe's way of telling each of us how special we are.

To look at the eye,
And marvel at how it works,
The magic and wonder of our senses,
Which give us the window into the reality we see,
What magic,
Pure magic.

And to think of all the things we know,
And all the things we don't know,
The opportunity to be able to comprehend reality seems heaven sent,
What an opportunity life can be,
If we take a moment to appreciate its splendour.

Life truly is a miracle,
Just how the body functions is a miracle,
The air we breathe,
Just rightly composed so we can breathe it and it sustain us,
What wonder,
What glorious wonder.

Sadness

Hovering,
Gnawing,
Eating away at my vitality,
Like being cocooned in a wet blanket on a cold day,
Miserable and dreary,
Why do you visit me, sadness?
Lingering like a bad dream.

Go away,
Leave me alone,
I want to feel joy,
To feel alive,
To feel excitement,
Not forlorn,
Go away sadness,
Let me be.

Peace

A word,
An idea,
A concept,
Do we even truly understand what it means?

The implications,
Is it something that's even achievable?
Is it something within the capacity of human beings?
Is it possible for us?
In our personal lives,
And at the greater scale of human social existence?
Or are we all too caught up in our own realities to be able to see someone else's reality?
For that is the ingredient for peace.

Can human beings as we are, achieve peace?
Or do we need to transcend to a higher level of consciousness?
As those who believe in war discover new ways to kill,
As nations bolster their armaments,
Deepen their understanding and commitment to the art of war,
As they ratchet up their rhetoric,
As some now speak of defending space,
Are we going to take our warring into the wider expanse of space?
Is this the destiny of humanity?

To fight,
Peace,
A word,
An idea,
A concept,
Do we even truly understand what it means?
Are we capable of it?
Can we transcend duality?

Them and us,
You versus the other,
Or is this our fundamental nature?
Our natural state of being,
What in fact makes us human.

Will we always let the things that divide us,
Beliefs, opinions, ideas, appearances, locations, rule the day?
It is clear to see,
That from on high,
All you see is one planet,
An astronaut can attest to that,
Astronauts, the testament to human potential,
Breaching our atmosphere,
Into the unknown of the cosmos,
Or are our divisions,
Our destiny?

Peace,
Is it a past time for idealists and dreamers?
The deluded?
An impracticality?
Or is it humanly possible?

Peace,
A word,
An idea,
A concept,
Is that all it can be?
Beyond the reach of the human condition?

Peace,
A word,
Or a possible reality,
What would the world look like?

Beauty

Our ability to perceive it,
Our ability to observe it,
Appreciate it,
Our ability to be entranced and enchanted by it,
Is one of the surest things that makes us human.

One of our sacred endowments,
From whatever thing that created us,
Our ability to think and feel in complex ways,
As our complex thoughts and complex emotions colour and impregnate our reality,
So, we can appreciate things like beauty in a complex and meaningful way.

What a privilege,
The test,
To be present to the beauty of reality more so than not.

Dusk

As the precisely crafted mechanics of the universe play themselves out,
As the seconds tick along,
The minutes,
And hours,
The clock work universe,
The sun has receded in the sky,
Waned in intensity and brightness,
Marking the beginning of the end of the day,
The great engine of the universe in full display.

Ticking along immaculately,
Elegantly,
Effortlessly,
Precisely,
So precise that our technology works because we can rely on this precision,
Rely on the dependability of the universe,
As time passes,
Another day is done,
Each moment a miracle,
Every second a miracle ever more so.

Dusk,
As the heavens signal to us that rest is nigh,
The end of the day draws closer,
Time to rest,
Weary celestial travellers.

Dawn

As day breaks,
And we wake up from our slumber,
Ready to be human again for another day,
As we wake up from our dreams,
Escape from our nightmares,
Our time spent in the subconscious,
With all the secrets it holds.

Wake up,
Dawn is here,
Day breaks,
The sun rises,
Ready to turn night into day,
Take us from the dark into the light.

Dawn,
A new day,
A new chance to be,
Another chance to experience life.

Dawn,
Wake up and win the day,
Wake up and live.

Ego

The big Me,
The I,
The thing that makes the human condition what it is,
The illusion that creates our reality,
The illusion of separation,
There is no life as we know it without the ego,
Self-determining,
Self-deluding,
Self-preserving.

Me,
The individual identity,
The very thing that makes us human,
Is also the very thing that's in the way,
Is it possible to transcend the ego?
Transcend it as a collective?

So powerful it is,
I must fulfil my ambitions,
See to my needs,
That is the human condition,
Is anything else possible?

Mother

Your love is like an ancient sacred scroll,
Teaching,
Showing,
Guiding,
Loving,
With the wisdom and the depth of the ages.

Your love is like a bottomless well,
A bustling, overflowing fountain,
You have taught me how to love,
How to be love,
How to show love,
How to care,
Care deeply,
With meaning and patience.

Your soul is old and wise,
It must have travelled through multiple lifetimes,
Learning the truth of life,
For the way you love shows you know the truth,
You know we are all connected,
More so than most.

The way you care,
Shows you know the meaning,
The true meaning of life,
And you have taught,
And you have shown,
For that's the true expression of love,
How its shown.

Even when you didn't have to,
You did,
When others wouldn't have,
You did even more so,
A sage you are,
For you know true wisdom,
The wisdom that is love.

Time

The irreducible constant,
The master of the universe,
The great onward march,
Inexorable,
The metronome of life,
The imperious overlord,
For they say time waits for no man,
And no man is greater than time,
Time conquers all,
There at the beginning,
If there ever was such a thing.

How to comprehend such a thing,
How to encapsulate such a thing,
How to articulate it,
Maybe some things are incommunicable,
Maybe even incomprehensible.

No matter how great we become,
No matter what we discover,
What we conquer,
What we achieve,
We will never conquer time.

A point to ponder,
As we work out our place in the universe,
Maybe the lesson there in,
Is to be humble.

War

Hate made manifest,
Killing made common place,
Killing normalised,
Bombs dropping from the sky,
Killing young and old alike,
Bullets ripping flesh,
Piercing and destroying organs,
Throats slashed,
Knives dripping with the blood of the fallen,
As the violent quench their blood lust.

Rape,
Human depravity,
Humanity at its most extreme.

War,
It's been our way since the dawn of mankind,
Will it also be the thing that sets the sun on mankind's time,
Brings our time to an end,
More so in this nuclear age,
This age of hyper and ever more complex technology.
If anything can end our time here on earth,
It's definitely war,
As it has done for countless souls in the past,

Seemingly aimless,
Pointless,
A failure to settle disputes,
Disputes which seem silly when history looks back,
Can we ever grow past war and fighting?
Can we ever transcend it?
The differences that divide us,
Will we ever see past them?

Bird

A hop,
And a skip,
And you are off,
Into the air,
Free to roam the skies,
Go where you please,
Looking at the world,
From on high,
Making a mockery of gravity.

Gravity,
What gravity,
That's for you humans to be concerned with,
To try and overcome,
Not me.

That's what you say with each effortless flap of your wings,
Gravity is no foe of mine,
I was built to conquer it,
To be with it,
The freedom to roam the skies,
Like the magnificent albatross,
Wings spread wide,
Gliding and floating through the skies,

Effortless and serene,
Majestic and triumphant.

Or the little sparrow,
Darting and zig zagging through the air,
A little miracle we witness,
Each time you take flight bird,
Us who are bound to the earth's surface,
Wed to it and beholden to the laws and dictates of gravity,
Unlike you bird,
Amazing you are.

Jazzman

Playing your mighty horn,
Telling your story,
Through melody and rhyme,
Turning air into joyous sound,
You puff your cheeks,
Blow and magic happens,
The sound of the soul.

You feel so deeply, jazzman,
Showing the depths of human emotion,
I hear what you are saying,
Even without words,
I feel it,
As your soul talks to mine,
This way,
I hear you more clearly,
Even more so than words would allow.

You speak of pain and life,
Love and joy,
You raise my spirit and reveal the depth,
The depth of consciousness and the human spirit.

Keep playing your tune jazzman,
Let my soul dance,
Don't ever stop.

Play on,
Play on.

Mighty jazzman,

Play on.

What Happens at the End

When you close your eyes for the last time,
When the lights switch off,
When the engine stops running,
It surely can't be the end,
All of this,
Just for nothing,
To be,
Then not be,
In an instant.

All we go through,
All we experience,
All that life is,
In every extraordinary extent of it,
The mountains,
The oceans,
The clouds in the sky,
The flora,
The fauna,
The moon,
The stars,
The planets,
The galaxies,
The universe,

And some even say,
The multiverse,
All of this to exist,
To be,
All for nothing.

All but to spend a brief moment on earth,
Then expire forever,
As if you were never here,
That surely can't be it,
To leave your loved ones behind,
And never see them again,
Surely, we meet again,
We must.

They say energy can't be destroyed,
It only changes form,
On that hope I cling,
That we just change in form,
And go elsewhere,
Maybe a glimpse into the truth,
That maybe we don't really perish,
Maybe it's the greatest deception,
The greatest illusion,
Life's infinite box of tricks.

Let us not be sad,
Let us rejoice,
Maybe friends,
Maybe we all meet again,
Maybe we meet those we love again,

Maybe the end,
Is only the beginning,
So be still.

Delivery

Fraught with risk and danger,
As ever,
Life and death in delicate balance,
The story of life,
Push, push,
Agony, ecstasy and expectation,
Such a toll on the body it takes,
The gift of life the resultant consequence.

Screams pierce the air,
Screams from the new born,
Shocked from suddenly being yanked from a place so comfortable and secure,
Welcome to the world.

Screams and shouts of joy too,
From those present to witness the miracle,
The miracle of birth,
The miracle of life,
The beginning of the road,
For a journey and destination unknown,
Welcome to the world little one,
Godspeed.

Serenity

Tranquillity,
Peace and calm,
Breathe.

All There Is, Is Space

Endless space,
Space and nothing,
Yet nothing can take form,
The wonder of the universe,
The miracle of creation,
All there is, is space,
Space and nothingness,
Intelligent space,
Intelligent nothingness,
Form,
The greatest illusion,
For all there is,
Is nothing.

We are All One

That is certainly true,
That is the ultimate truth,
We do,
Don't we,
Look at the same sun,
See the same stars,
Observe the same moon,
Walk the same earth,
Eat food to live.

We pretend,
And pretend so well,
To act as though we are not one,
To live as though we are not one,
We have mastered it over the ages,
But the truth is inescapable,
We are all one.

Are we not all created the same way,
A man and a woman must meet,
Delivered the same way,
A woman must labour,
Nursed the same way,
Is this not true?

It certainly is,
That cannot be denied,
Shall we keep pretending,
Will we keep pretending,
Pretending not to know,
That we are all one.

It's All Truth

It's all light,
And we are but mirrors,
Prisms,
Surfaces of a rough-cut diamond,
Reflecting the light in our own unique way,
But it's all truth,
It's all light.

We are all pieces and fragments of that truth,
We all see the truth,
See the light,
In our own personal ways,
But it's all truth,
It's all light,
Look for the light shining in every one of us,
It's there.

Duality

The Dichotic dilemma,
Them, us,
Him, her,
Love, hate,
Up, down,
War, peace,
Good, bad,
Socialism, capitalism,
Knowledge, ignorance,
Patience, impatience,
Black, white.

The very stitching of our reality,
The very fabric that makes it,
Our reality as we know it wouldn't exist without it.

Racism, racial harmony,
Power and a lack of it,
Greed and corruption,
Wisdom and righthood,
Our very consciousness revolves around duality,
Asleep, awake,
Conscious, unconscious,
Freedom and a lack of it.

Is this our fate and destiny?
Or something we can transcend,
We seem designed,
Engineered to precision to see the world this way,
For the world to be this way.

Fat, thin,
Short, tall,
We only understand reality because opposites exist,
We would not be able to perceive good if bad didn't exist,
We wouldn't be able to value life if death did not exist,
The cause of all our problems is most always the solution to all our problems.

Duality,
The Dichotic dilemma,
Is anything else possible,
Or is this all life can ever be?
Is this all life is?

Nelson Mandela

You said enough is enough,
I will see freedom for my people,
In my lifetime,
And you did,
When a powerful and brutal system said you were not equal,
You said I am,
You said we are,
You spoke to minds that were already made up,
You spoke to hearts that were not willing to be turned or softened.

Yet those minds you convinced,
And those hearts you turned and softened,
Though not all,
But enough such that there could be change,
The rest you left to us,
Those that followed in your footsteps.

You gave the best years of your life to struggle,
You were one of those that would not stand idly by,
You were one of those sent to lead,
Sent to be an example,
Sent to swim against powerful currents,
With indefatigable will and spirit.

Like the salmon,
On its great run,
Swim till the deed is done,
And the deed was done.

And like a true leader,
A true visionary,
A true Statesman,
A true father of a nation,
You said my part is done,
Now the rest is up to you.

And it is,
For one person can't do it all by themselves,
It's not up to just one individual,
We must all do our part,
You relinquished power,
Like a true wise man,
Setting an example,
A legacy,
Being the example for others to follow,
For you knew it wasn't about power,
It was about freedom,
It was about more.

And your last days were spent happy,
Singing and dancing,
For you had gone through the eye of the needle,
You had transcended duality,
You saw past the smallness of human struggle and strife,
You had met God.

Seen into the light,
Through the darkness,
And you were the light,
That's why all loved you in the end,
Most anyway,
Especially those who had hated you before,
Brought a truly divided nation together,
Performed a mass healing,
In a gaping chasm of a wound of the human psyche.

And I'm sure when you closed your eyes for the last time,
When you got to the other side,
They opened and you discovered you had already been there,
May your example continue to inform us,
Great traveller.

Martin Luther King

You had a dream,
Through the darkest times,
Through the most impossible odds,
You never lost sight of your dream,
You saw through the mist and fog of human confusion,
When they threw rocks at you,
You said love and peace is the way.

With just the power of words,
The power of persuasion,
The power of good intention,
You managed to bring change to the world,
You were a true warrior of light,
A man of vision,
Saintly.

Countless souls experience better days thanks to your efforts,
And for that you gave your life,
Your life was taken,
By those who are blinded by the light,
Yet your bright flame burns on,
The light of your words still shines to this day,
And will always shine,
Your legacy becoming ever stronger with each passing day.

And yet more work needs to be done,
For had you been allowed more time on this earth,
We will have learnt more of what your great mind saw,
What your great soul sought,
Yet more light of truth might have been beamed into the earth through you,
As you grew more,
Learnt more,
And saw more.

Yet what you did was still more than enough,
A life well lived,
A destiny well fulfilled,
A life of purpose exemplified,
On the shoulders of giants we stand,
And you sir were more than a giant,
You were a titan,
A demigod,
A true warrior of light.

Dark in Complexion

Dark in skin,
Cast into the shadows,
Cast into the shadows of life,
Cast into the shadows of history,
Living in the shadows,
Living in the ghettos,
And fighting to come into the light,
Into the sun and out of the shadows.

Dark in skin and dark in complexion,
Show me your train ticket,
But sir, you are not checking everyone else's,
All I am trying to do is get to my destination,
Dark in skin,
Dark in complexion,
And living in the shadows.

From the land where the sun burns bright,
Shines brightest,
Darkening the skin,
Darkening the complexion,
Yet the people live in the shadows,
In others' shadows,
In the land where the sun shines brightest.

The ironies of life,
Dark in skin,
Dark in complexion,
Yet they smile,
Smile wide and smile bright,
Radiating the sun,
The sun that shines and burns from within,
Dark in skin,
Dark in complexion.

Migrant

Refugee,
In boats and such,
Across seas,
Across land,
Perilous journeys,
To destinies unknown,
Your fate not your own,
Your fate in the hands of others,
Seeking a better life,
Fleeing danger,
Fuelled by hopes, dreams and aspirations.

Some hate you migrant,
Some hate you refugee,
A scourge,
A swarm,
An invasion
Some say,
Dark skin tones characterise most of you,
Reflecting the state of the world,
Reflecting the history of the world.

Some hate you migrant,
Some hate you refugee,
Unwanted you are.

How about we just heal the world,
Would that not solve our problems,
A world with no more migrants,
No more refugees,
Just expats,
Expats and tourists.

How much different is the expat, the tourist,
From the migrant, the refugee?
Is not what drives them the same?
Yet what divides them is necessity and privilege,
One is driven by necessity,
One is driven by privilege,
But what they seek is the same,
A better life in foreign lands,
To get more out of life,
The illusion of separation.

Love and loving

Sweet,
Warm,
Gentle,
Tender,
Kind,
Strong,
Patient.

African

Singing,
Dancing,
Ululating,
That is your way,
Exuberant,
Expressive,
Flamboyant,
Colourful,
With smiles as wide as the sea,
And as warm as the sun,
Despite it all,
Despite it all.

You have a joy for life,
An excitement that's infectious,
You laugh so loud,
And laugh so true,
As though all is well in the world,
Such warmth,
And the beauty of your land,
Enchanting,
Your customs,
Your hidden secrets,
Your mysteries,

Your story that's not yet been told,
What ancient wisdoms do you hold?

The xylophone,
The mbira,
The kora,
Your melody,
Your sound,
Truly enchanting.

The drum,
The beating heart of Africa,
Telling a story as ancient as time itself,
A rhythm,
A pulsating rhythm,
The mighty beasts,
Africa,
You are beautiful.

Patrice Lumumba

I moan your loss,
Oh, where would Africa be today had, the revolutionary leaders been allowed to lead?
Had they not been killed.

Thomas Sankara too.

The burning desire for progress roars within her,
Africa,
The bright minds linger within her,
The agents of change aplenty,
Yet they won't set her free because she has diamonds, gold, platinum and every manner of riches,
Will they ever set her free?
Will they ever set her people free?

God

Eternal,
Certainly,
Outside of time,
Incomprehensibly so,
Beyond cognition,
Beyond imagine,
All encompassing,
Incommunicable.

Intelligent,
Alive,
Beyond what's perceivable with the human mind,
Leaves us to be,
As an expression of true love,
The gift of being human.

So, what can we be?
Fighting and hating for eternity,
Or can we be more?
Racism,
Hatred,
And all these small things,
Or can humanity become present to the grandeur of existence?
The true grandeur of God,

The true grandeur of life,
The remarkable opportunity it is to be alive,
To be you.

How do you choose to spend that opportunity?
Being someone spreading hatred and misery,
Or spreading love,
Being small,
Or being great,
Because love is what's great about being alive,
Being Godly,
Because God is love.

We are all Human Beings

That is certainly true,
Every last one of us,
If you are birthed from your mother's womb,
You are certainly human,
How so ever you present,
Black,
White,
Asian,
Israeli,
Palestinian.

Able bodied,
Disabled,
Your politics,
Your religion,
Your beliefs,
And in this day and age,
However you identify,
All human,
That is certainly true.

The architects of racial division knew this,
That's why they head to teach racial division,
And masterful they were,

That's how they could justify their systems of oppression and exploitation,
The echoes, reverberations and ramifications of which we still live with today,
But the truth is,
We are all human.

We should be wary of those who seek to divide us,
They are exploiters and progenitors of so much suffering and pain,
All our suffering comes when we don't acknowledge each other's humanity,
When indeed the truth is,
We are all human,
Racism hatred and exploitation,
These are the lowest forms of human self-expression,
The lowest forms of consciousness.

Humanity

Enemies, friends,
Love, hate,
The many faces we wear in this intricate dance called life,
How we sway every day,
Back and forth between love and hatred,
Love and hatred,
For your wife,
Your brother,
Your mother,
Your neighbour,
Your countrymen,
Those from other countries,
The world,
The other,
Even yourself.

All in the intricate web we call our life,
How incredible it all is to ponder,
How engrossing and convincing it is,
When hate courses through you like a raging fire,
Or when love cocoons and envelopes you in its warm embrace,
How deluding it all is,
Maybe all for a moment.

Just a moment of clarity,
When the truth shines in,
The truth of the totality of it all,
That it's all a passing phase,
And maybe one day you get to bask in the eternal truth of the oneness of it all.

How that person you thought was an enemy truly and really is not,
How you missed and were missing all the beauty that they possess,
All the beauty that they see,
And all the beauty that they are,
And that in the end they were no different from you,
Not even in the slightest.

Oh, what a majestic and wondrous game we play,
This mesmerising illusion,
This thing we call life,
Weaving its web,
Its intricate web of smoke and mirrors,
Deceiving and deluding us from seeing the eternal truth,
That we are truly not different,
The beauty and the love that lives in you,
Also lives in the other.

Will I Ever Find My True Love

The quest of a true romantic,
The journey of a true romantic,
The fate of a true romantic,
The search for true love,
That other person to be the fulfilment of love,
The fulfilment of all that love promises,
The story that's been told,
Since we began telling stories.

Ageless,
The search for love,
Will I find you,
That other person that makes it all worth it,
The days of loneliness,
Wishing,
Dreaming,
Yearning,
And hoping,
To complete the circle.

What a joyous day it will be,
When the heart says yes, that's the one,
When destiny plays its hand,
When fate fulfils its mission,

The fantasy of a hopeless dreamer,
But it's the dreamers who achieve the truly great things,
Live the truly great lives,
See the most truly awe-inspiring things in their hearts and in their minds,
They dream the impossible when it seems impossible.

Its dreams that can bring heaven down to earth,
So, dream the dream of love,
I will dream it,
I will be a hopeless dreamer,
A hopeless romantic,
Till the daydreams become reality,
And oh, what a day it will be,
When dreams become reality,
It is the thing that makes life truly worth living.

Will I ever find you my true love?
It matters not though,
For while I wait,
I see you in my dreams,
And I live with you in my hopes and fantasies,
Till the day we meet.

Freedom

Freedom to be,
Freedom to sing,
Freedom to express,
Express one's self,
Freedom to dance,
Freedom to learn,
Learn what the mind wants to know,
Freedom just to be.

Could there be a more precious thing?
Those who may take freedom from others,
Are light stealers,
For freedom is light,
Light radiating the expression of the soul,
Let freedom reign,
Let the human soul be free,
Unbound,
Free to be.

Life is a unique and special opportunity to be,
And only the one opportunity you are granted as you, to be you,
So yes,
Let freedom reign,
Let the human soul be free.

Tree

Stretching up into the heavens,
Searching for the sun's rays,
Your roots planted deep into the earth,
A network,
A web of tentacles in the earth.

Tree,
You breathe out,
What we breathe in,
What symbiosis,
What design.

Only but a seed you once were,
The potential for all you are, trapped within,
Magic.

Planted into the soil you were,
Nurtured by Gaia,
The mother,
The mother of all,
The all mother,
Mother to all of us,
The great nurturer,
The great provider,

Earth.
And from her you burst,
Burst forth into what you are,
Strong and sturdy,
A giant reaching to the heavens,
There to stand for years,
Hundreds,
Maybe even thousands,
Like a sentry,
A guard,
Watching time go by,
The days,
Months,
Years,
Epochs.

Keeping a watchful eye,
Steady and still,
But for the wind,
Rocking you back and forth,
Moving your branches,
Blowing away the leaves,
Spreading the seeds,
Your seed,
What a marvel,
Just to look at you, tree,
And be amazed at what you are.

Choice

It's all programming,
Emotion,
Instinct,
Social conditioning,
Innate drives and preconditions,
But then there is choice.

Choice is the point of human consciousness,
The distinguishing human characteristic,
It is the thing that makes us human,
The power to choose,
The opportunity to choose,
And it is what we choose that determines life,
Determines existence.

How much say does one have in the matter?
In light of all that governs us,
To say none is to say we are perhaps soulless automatons,
So, one can say then that yes,
Human choice is real,
And if so,
Then our destiny is in our hands,
An empowering thought,
Then the question is,
Are we capable of making the right choices?

In our own lives and as humanity,
To choose the light or choose the dark,
Love or hate,
And everything else.

It is fair to say,
In the mist and fog of it all,
In the mist and fog of life,
There are moments of lucidity,
Moments of clarity,
And it's in those moments where we get to be human,
Where we get to choose.

For when rage consumes,
And hate overpowers,
And the emotions flood,
How much choice does one have?
A point to ponder,
Yet in the end,
One must conclude to say,
We still have the power to choose,
Else what are we?

I Embrace the Loneliness

The solitude,
I welcome it,
Once with reluctant arms,
But now with open arms,
I see it for what it is now,
An opportunity for peace,
An opportunity for silence,
An opportunity for meditation,
Contemplation.

To commune with God,
To commune with the universe,
Straighten out the thoughts,
The emotions,
Visit those dark corners that you don't reach when life is busy,
Meet them,
See them,
Be challenged by them,
Learn from them,
See what's there,
Be with it,
I welcome you,
Loneliness.

We are Made in God's Image

God the Universe,
For they tell us that the Universe is always expanding,
But so are we,
Look at love,
Look at emotion,
But love in this case,
It can grow and grow and grow,
Expand infinitely.

The love you have for your child,
Captivated by the idea of them before they are even here,
Whilst they live in your fantasies, you love them,
When they are conceived you love them even more,
Then when they are born your love explodes like the big bang,
Spawning new life,
New possibilities,
An entirely new Universe of possibility.

Then when they cry your love grows and expands,
When they are sick, your love grows and expands even more,
Ever more so,
Ever more so like the expanding Universe,
Then they crawl,
Take their first steps,

And speak words for the first time,
Your love grows and expands more still.
Then you discover them as their mind develops,
As their grasp of life and existence expands,
You hear their thoughts,
Their desires,
Their wishes,
And your love grows and expands still,
Just like the Universe.

Then you watch them become adults,
Walk side by side with you,
Stride for stride and grow into who they will be,
Your love and admiration grows and expands even greater,
As it becomes love, pride and many other things,
Then you experience them through life,
Till your dying day,
Love growing and expanding ever more so,
Just like the Universe,
In God's image we are created,
Yes, indeed we are.

Unconditional Love

The power to accept all that is,
The insight to see all that is,
The wisdom to understand it all,
That's unconditional love,
Why is there suffering?
Why is there misery?
Why is there death?

Unconditional love,
The deepest insight of life,
The unfurling of reality,
The true nature of reality,
The ability to see,
To truly see,
To know,
To truly know.

Unconditional love,
Life's noble journey,
The true destination,
The place where one can be with all of reality,
And truly get it,
Unconditional love,
The gateway to real peace.

Love and Pain

Go hand in hand,
Forever intertwined,
Like ill-fated lovers,
Star crossed lovers,
Forever flowing together,
Manifesting together,
As though that's how it is meant to be.

Where there is love there is pain,
Or there will be pain,
A strange irony,
A strange state of play,
For we search for love,
In search of happiness,
Yet that happiness,
Invariably comes with pain,
Where there is love there is also suffering.

The most pain you can experience,
Is the pain caused by love,
The pain when you are in love,
The pain caused by those who love too much,
Love their own land,
Their own people.

How strange,
For love is meant to bring happiness,
Yet it can bring so much pain and suffering,
The lesson there in,
Hard to decipher.

Maybe that love is pain,
Where there is love,
There is pain,
Where there is life,
There is pain,
Hard to accept,
But the truth seems hard to deny,
For we do suffer in this life,
We do feel pain,
Especially the pain love causes,
All there is to do,
Is to contemplate deeper.

It Really Doesn't Matter

Because we are all going to die anyway,
And death is beautiful,
So, all the things we fight for,
Dominance,
Power,
All the fighting we do,
All the righthood we seek,
It really doesn't matter,
Because in the end,
We all die anyway.

So why not love instead,
But not just a limited love,
A selfish love,
A self-centred love,
An egocentric love,
A love confined just to what you know,
What you identify with,
But instead,
Love it all,
Expand your love,
Grow your love,
Love that which seems separate to you,
Alien to you,

Wrong to you,
Love it.

Of course, you can hate,
That's what it is to be human,
The freedom and the ability to,
But why not try love,
It's a better journey,
It's a greater journey,
The destination is the better one,
For everyone,
It may be the harder journey,
But it's the more inspired journey.

That which seems foreign,
Is just an accident of birth,
That could have been you,
What a thought.

What is identity?
But a set of learnt values and beliefs,
When the greatest and clearest identity,
Is that we are all human,
So yes,
In the end,
It really doesn't matter,
Everything that we think is important,
Because in time,
It's all left behind,
So why not love instead,
In the greatest possible way.

Suffering

We all suffer,
Every person suffers,
Yes, it's all relative,
It can be and is relative,
But we all suffer,
Rich or poor,
Black or white,
No matter the colour,
No matter where you come from,
To be human,
Is to suffer,
No one escapes.

So, when the dark times come,
Know you are not alone,
It's not just you,
It's the human condition,
It seems suffering is part of what we must do here,
Some say there is a purpose,
Another life to be lived after this one is done,
So maybe we suffer here,
So that we don't suffer there,
For sure there is happiness here too,
Which is good,

But there certainly also is suffering,
No one escapes that.
It's a unifying truth,
We will and all suffer in some way,
So indeed, when the dark times come,
When the dark clouds descend,
Know you are not alone.

Melancholy

The complexity of human emotion,
The complexity of the human condition,
As the human emotional engine churns,
A feeling of pensive sadness overwhelms,
Melancholy,
To feel this is to be human,
Is to be present to the wonder of what we are,
Even, to wonder at what we are,
Wonder what we are doing here,
Such that one should feel melancholic,
One can feel melancholic,
Experience melancholy.

As the feeling colours your reality,
And you wonder why you feel like this,
Why do I feel like this?
Why should I feel like this?
As thoughts and memories conspire,
Conspire to create this feeling of pensive sadness,
Melancholy,
The human condition,
Wonderment and bewilderment,
It's amazing what we are.

These strange creatures,
These strange thinking and feeling creatures,
Emotions,
Melancholy,
Such a mystery,
The mystery of life,
What would conspire to make this?
Make us,
Make us the way we are.

These weird and wonderful creatures,
Thinking, talking and feeling creatures,
Able to perceive and experience so much,
So broadly,
So greatly,
So deeply,
Melancholy being one such deep emotion,
The human condition,
Weird and bizarre,
Weird and awe inspiring.

The Joy of Parenthood

One of life's great endeavours,
One of life's challenges and aims,
Is to live a life with purpose,
Through parenthood thus,
Purpose comes wrapped up in a little bundle you call your child.

All of a sudden,
A life that could have seemed meaningless,
Now has meaning,
Problems that seemed insurmountable and all consuming,
Move to the periphery,
There is a new focus,
A new determination,
A certain completeness,
A reminder of the grandeur of life,
The wonder of existence.

Every time you see your child,
How this thing exists,
Only because of you,
There couldn't be a deeper miracle in all of creation,
Flesh made from your flesh,
A piece of you.

A true miracle,
An opportunity to deepen your understanding of life and love,
As you overcome your natural instinct to self-preserve,
As the needs of another take precedent over your own,
All the lessons of life and love wrapped up in the form of your child,
The joy of parenthood,
A labour of love,
You labour to deliver them into the world,
Then labour to look after them,
This is life,
This is love.

And through a child,
You are given something to love unconditionally,
And that's the deepest gift of parenthood,
An opportunity to learn unconditional love,
And that is the joy of parenthood,
The challenge of parenthood,
An opportunity to learn to love through it all,
Through all the tribulations,
And despite all the challenges,
A lesson we should learn and extend outwards.

This life

Undulating,
Circuitous,
A maze,
Undulating as we deal with the up and down nature of our fate and emotions,
Circuitous as the road to our destination is so full of twists and turns,
A maze of conflicting emotions and circumstances.

It's beautiful though,
Beautiful in its pain and mystery,
Beautiful in its pain and wonder,
But beautiful it is,
Yet it all can seem meaningless,
Empty and meaningless,
For we come,
We toil,
Then we expire,
Seemingly with no cause or purpose,
Except for the beliefs and theories, we have amassed over time.

But the real truth,
The actual truth,

No one knows,
For once you leave,
There is no way back,
There is no way to come and report back on what was on the other side,
It's a one-way ticket it seems.

So, all we are left to do is to wonder,
All we are left with is the wonder,
The wonder of how such a thing exists,
Such a thing as life,
The wonder of how even anything exists,
And yet exist it does,
All the millions of life forms,
All the billions of stars and galaxies,
The robbers,
The thieves,
The scoundrels and reprobates,
The plankton,
The microscopic creatures.

All that we have discovered,
And yet to discover,
And will never discover,
It all exists,
Reality exists,
It's amazing,
It's beautiful,
And it's real,
At times it's too real,
As the brutality of life manifests itself,

And yet, it's that brutality that proves,
Proves that life is truly real,
Makes life viscerally real,
And it's that brutality that makes the beauty of life possible,
For you can't have one without the other,
There must be a truth in that,
There must be an ultimate truth in there somewhere,
And it's when you can see the beauty in the brutality,
That you can see the beauty in everything,
The beauty in all of it,
The ultimate beauty.

Second Class Citizen

That's my fate,
That's my inheritance,
I must live with that,
That's what I have to live with,
Yes, you have to live with the inheritance of being called a villain,
Of being the villain,
In our recent history,
Yes, that's your inheritance,
It's something you must grapple with,
But that's all it is,
Something you must grapple with.

But try grappling with being a second-class citizen,
Try having to live that reality,
That in this wondrous existence,
Mine gets to be the life of a second-class citizen,
How your very defining characteristics are a barrier for you,
Create barriers for you,
And presumptions about you,
Often negative ones.

How your very defining characteristics endowed by God itself,

Mark you,
And follow you,
And remind you that in this time,
You are a second-class citizen,
And everywhere you go,
Everything reminds you of this,
When you see the impoverishment of those who look like you,
When you see the disenfranchisement of those who look like you.

As opposed to your position of relative opulence,
And indeed, yes, your privilege,
Yes, you get to be the villain of our time,
But I get to be the second-class citizen,
I get to live with that,
You don't.

As the football hooligans remind me when I step on the pitch,
And the little slights I experience,
The gentle reminders,
And the sometimes not so gentle ones,
I inherited a reality where a whole complex system was designed to oppress me and tell me I am less than.

Science,
Politics,
Economics,
Religion.

All structured and designed to reinforce my inferiority,
Have things changed?

Are things moving forward?
Of course, yes,
But is this still my inheritance?
Yes,
And your inheritance too,
So, when they say white privilege,
This is what they mean,
Your inheritance from history,
Versus my inheritance from history,
And in that,
There is no confusion,
Our recent history is very clear,
And our social and historical inheritance is very clear.

So, what to do about it?
Well, what we can do,
Is abandon our camps,
Abandon the positions we have taken up to defend,
Accept that we all sin,
History is history,
And come together.

No One is Wrong Really

In the strictest sense,
The nationalist,
The so-called terrorist,
The racist,
The xenophobe,
The socialist,
The communist,
The capitalist,
The Marxist.

No one is wrong really,
Shades of grey,
That's all life is,
Shades of grey,
This is life's primary colour,
They all see some truth,
Espouse some truth,
Come from some version of the truth,
A truth that they see,
That is the truth,
That it's all relative truth.

That's all we have,
Partial glimpses,

Based on what we learn,
And what life calls us to believe in,
Yet they are all united by one thing,
They hold their truths as the absolute truth.

That is where they fail,
For if they saw the real truth,
The ultimate truth,
They would know that theirs is only partial,
And when we hold onto these partial truths,
As though they were the ultimate truth,
We deny the truth that others see.

Their truths too are true,
So, what's the ultimate truth then?
Well as ever,
The ultimate truth,
Is the truth of oneness,
That is the only real truth,
Not partial truth,
But ultimate absolute truth.

And when you see this,
You see all the light,
Not the partial light,
And you know for sure,
That all truths are true,
But only partially true,
Except the one truth.

Music

The analgesia to the soul,
Telling us that truly all is well,
In the place where inspiration comes from,
In the place where we all come from,
It is well.

Music,
A panacea,
If only for a moment,
The moment and moments,
When you are swept away,
Swept away and lost,
Lost in the beat,
The harmony,
The lyrics,
The flow,
The melody.

In that moment of dancing,
That moment of appreciation,
Lost in the transportive quality of music,
It is all well,
It is all well in the world.

There is no suffering,
In that moment,

No sorrow,
No misery,
No angst,
Just joy,
Joy and celebration,
Joyful celebration.

Music,
The analgesia to the soul,
The panacea to life's ills,
If only for a moment,
But that too is fine,
Because life after all is about moments.

Music,
Sourced right from source,
No wonder we are enamoured by it,
Entranced by it,
Enchanted by it,
Moved by it.

Communicating a deeper truth,
A truth that is beautiful,
That behind the veil,
The illusory veil of life,
It is all beautiful,
Heal my soul music,
Speak to my soul,
The analgesia,
The panacea,
To the soul.

Like a Phoenix I Rise

From the smouldering cinders of ruin and destruction I rise,
Battered and bruised,
Beaten and trampled on,
By the cruel fate of destiny,
And the unforgiving relentlessness of misfortune,
Despite it all I rise.

I wonder,
What unbreakable spirit lives inside of me,
What indefatigable will and drive,
Insurmountable capacity for hope,
Even in the darkest despair,
Is this my strength thy heavens?
Is this the gift you have given me?
The gift to endure.

When the darkness came for me,
And surrounded me at every turn and was everywhere I looked,
No light shone,
Except the light from within,
The light from my unbreakable will.

So, throw your worst at me fate,
Do your worst,
Do your best,
For here you will find a warrior,
Ready for battle,
Built to withstand the highest heat,
And the most arduous of circumstances.

And when the flames descend,
And I am trampled and defeated,
Know this,
In the end,
From the ashes,
I will rise.

White Privilege

A nebulous concept,
A divisive concept,
Controversial and perhaps toxic,
A schism,
A schism between those who are called black and those who are called white.

And it exists because,
In times gone by,
Some of those who are called white decided that,
Those who are called black are the lowest of the low,
Even subhuman,
Non-human.

Some deny white privilege,
Recoil at the very mention of the thing,
There is no such thing they say,
A spurious concept born from an inferiority complex,
But I say,
To deny it,
Is to deny history itself,
To deny history and the present reality it creates,
The future it creates.

For the reality is we live in different worlds you and I,
I for my black skin see a different world,
And you for your white skin see a different world,
And the world sees us differently,
Responds differently to each of us,
The whole world puts us in different places you and I,
You in a higher place and me in a lower place,
To deny the reality of white privilege,
Is to deny the hard work,
Deep thinking and strategizing,
Done by some of those of white skin who so conclusively conquered the world.

And yes, they did,
And they birthed a new world,
This world we live in today,
White privilege was the desired outcome of their hard work,
To deny this is to deny their very efforts,
Of course, today,
This leaves a sour taste in the mouth,
So, it is denied and obfuscated,
Some try to deny, expunge or whitewash,
The harsh truths of conquest,
And in doing so,
Break the link between the past and the present,
And in doing so deny that white privilege exists,
Is a real phenomenon.

At times by pointing to the existence of economically deprived white people,

The existence of economically deprived white people is a phenomenon of class and individual circumstance,
But white privilege is a more sweeping and intrinsic phenomenon to society than just economics.

It's the social fabric of a society and world which was built on promoting whiteness as greater than all,
And the resulting world we live in today where whiteness still has inherent benefits in society over all others but especially blacks,
This is the essence of white privilege,
It transcends economic or educational status and is purely about how the world sees you based purely on the colour of your skin,
The inherent advantage of being white in the world.

White privilege was the intended outcome of centuries of hard work,
So, you can't deny it today,
Because you think it makes you look like a villain,
When you want to look like the hero,
The good guys.

The truth though is, however,
We all can be heroes and we all can be villains,
We all can be good or bad,
This is what it is to be human.

Accepting the reality of white privilege,
Is accepting the reality of history,
The day we can make peace with that,

Is the day we can move forward from this dark history as one.

White privilege is the very embodiment and reality of history,
Everything that's good about it,
And everything that's bad about it,
Hence,
Let's abandon denialism,
Let's abandon recriminations,
We all sin,
Human progress and life are very strange things,
The question then is,
How do we move on together?

All There is, is Us

Human beings,
We are all there is,
We are all that's in the way,
And we are the way.

The fighting,
The wars,
Us,
The disagreements,
The misunderstandings,
Us,
Who is right,
Who is wrong,
Us,
Communism, socialism or capitalism,
Us.

America,
Or China,
Or Russia,
Islam or Christianity,
Black or white,
All the schisms of the world,
It's all us.

Human beings,
We are all that's in the way,
The fighting we do,
The disagreements,
The quarrelling,
The hating,
The killing,
It's all us.

Imagine,
Just imagine if we somehow got over it,
Got over ourselves,
Managed to get along,
Maybe just for one day,
Maybe a week,
A month,
A year,
Imagine what we could create,
If we just got along,
Saw eye to eye,
Just for a moment.

Global warming,
Financial crisis,
Poverty,
War,
If we got along,
We would be able to answer all these questions,
Solve all these problems,
Imagine if we all saw,
Just for a moment,

That all there is here is us,
We rule the roost,
No one else,
This Kingdom,
This plain of existence we were given,
To be Kings and Queens,
Overlords,
Lords of the Manor,
We rule this plain,
Everything is down to us,
What an opportunity.

Yet we squander it,
Fighting,
Killing,
Disagreeing,
Being selfish,
Looking after what we consider our own,
When it's all ours here,
Everything,
It's all ours.

Take away all the divisions and barriers,
Then it's plain to see,
That these words are true,
That it's just us here,
And what we create,
What could we create?
Create together,
If and when we truly got,
That, it's just us here.

The Communist, the Socialist and the Capitalist

Like sworn enemies they are,
Destined to be at odds,
Forever it seems,
Their values and ideals,
Seemingly at loggerheads.

Yet in actuality,
They are saying the same thing,
The Communist is saying everyone matters equally,
And we should meet the needs of all,
And the Capitalist is saying every individual matters,
And we should meet the needs of each individual,
The individual is sacrosanct,
So, in principle,
The assertions and fundamental positions are tantamount to the same thing,
They are both attesting to the worth and value of everyone,
Though approaching from different lenses,
So why can't they see this?

The Communist and the socialist sees the suffering of the masses,

And says we must look after the masses,
Every individual matters,
Yet the capitalist says we must enrich the individual,
We must enshrine the rights of the individual,
Every individual matters,
So, I say again,
In principle they are saying the same thing.

Of course, how they get there each is a different story,
And for that they fight,
But it's clear to see that the intentions of both are good,
That certainly is true,
Yet they will demonise each other,
The other arguing how evil the other is,
Yet the truth is both systems have blood on their hands,
The nations who have called themselves communist and socialist,
And the nations who have called themselves capitalist,
All have blood on their hands,
The historical record is clear.

The implementation of both systems has brought suffering for others,
The historical record is clear on this as well,
So, won't the proponents and devout believers of each system see this,
Probably not,
It's much easier to vilify than unify,
For it seems it's in our nature to fight,
We would rather go to war and hate over our ideologies and disagreements than come to an understanding,

It seems this is the nature of humanity,
When what we fight for and kill for is differences in opinion,
Differences in perspective,
Of course, yes, so much rides on those differences.

But can we be greater than those differences?
Look for the good rather than the bad in the other,
See the wholeness of it rather than the separation,
Appreciate what's on the other side as much as what's on your side,
It seems simple enough.

Yet the last thing we seem to be is simple,
The solutions seem simple enough,
Yet getting there seems impossible,
The dream of a better world,
A dreamer's fantasy,
A world that works in the best interests of all.

Everyone Must Rest

It is the way,
Even though I love you so,
I know you must go,
Everyone must rest,
It certainly is nature's way,
The cycle of life and death.

You came so I could be,
Because of you,
I am,
Yet one day,
You must leave this plain,
Leave me alone,
And it hurts me so,
Just the thought of it,
Let alone one day,
Living the reality of it.

But it is so,
We come and we must go,
It is the way,
For all living creatures,
And this we are,
As surely as the seasons come and go,

We too,
Must come and we must go.

But I know as beautiful as you are,
You will certainly go to a beautiful place,
And maybe one day,
I will meet you there again,
When my time to go,
Also comes,
For this is the way,
Just as the sun must rise and set,
We too must rise and be set to rest,
Even though it hurts me so,
It is the way it must go.

We are the Question

And we are the answer,
Us beings,
Human beings,
What is the greatest sense of ourselves we can have?
Is it the individual?
Is it the collective?
Is it nationhood?
Or is it the realisation of the oneness of it all.

We are the answer,
And we are the question,
Poverty,
War,
Hatred,
Love,
Peace,
Togetherness,
Enmity.

We are the answer,
We are the question,
We are the question,
And we are the answer,
Us beings,
Human beings.

Global Warming

Climate change,
Finite resources,
War,
The dark spectres we face,
The dark spectres that threaten our very existence,
The challenges we face as a species,
The very existential realities that could affect human life irrevocably,
Some even say we face our extinction.

Yet as they cry out from the darkness for change,
Some see inaction,
Business as usual,
The ratcheting up of tensions,
No change,
Or not enough of it,
The pace of it too slow,
Much like the antelope grazing in the savannah,
The gazelle,
Knows the lion is close by,
The cheetah,
The leopard,
It can smell it in the air,
Sense it in the ether,

As it looks up pensively,
Every now and again,
But goes back to grazing,
As the predator lurks,
Approaches,
Stealthily,
Insidiously,
Until it's too late for the gazelle,
The antelope,
And it's caught in the fangs,
The razor-sharp claws,
A death grip that it can't escape.

So might it be for us,
With these challenges we face,
Yet on the other hand,
Fate seems to be in our hands,
At least for now,
Yet we disagree,
Disagree and disagree,
When it seems simple enough to say unity is the answer,
Maybe it's simple enough for a poet to say,
When maybe life just isn't that simple,
Yet one feels compelled to say,
Feels its right to say,
Unity is the answer,
Can we not put our differences aside?
For a greater vision.

Mixed Race Child

Born of two worlds,
Your existence is life's deepest lesson,
For where others try and teach difference,
Try and teach separation,
Your very existence shatters the myths and untruths.

Mixed race child,
Your heritage is complex,
Straddling two realities,
Trying to make sense of who you are,
Make sense of what you are in this complex and divided world.

But I'll tell you what you are,
I'll tell you this,
You are human,
Perfect, whole and complete,
You prove the humanity in all of us.

In bygone days,
When those who believe in harmful separation feared the races mixing,
As worlds collided,
Miscegenation they said,

You came into the world,
And even then,
You proved the humanity in us all.

Mixed race child,
You are beautiful,
Not only because you are mixed,
But mostly because you prove the humanity in all of us,
You prove those that would tell us we are different,
We should be separate,
Stick to our own,
Some are more human than others,
You prove that they are liars.

You prove that we are all human,
And for this,
Mixed race child,
You are truly beautiful.
You tell the deepest story about being human.

Can We Reinvent Humanity

Redefine what it means to be a human being,
Invent an idea of ourselves that speaks to what an incredible manifestation it is to be a human being,
We have and do,
Define ourselves through narrow lenses,
Lenses of location and tribe,
Creed and culture,
Beliefs, political, religious.

Yes, these are real,
And they connect us to something,
But can we connect to something more?
Something greater,
We define ourselves mostly,
Based on how we are different from each other,
And these differences are real,
But how can we transcend these?
Transcend these in a way that brings humanity together,
Not set us asunder,
To loot and plunder.

So, as time ticks on,
And the past and history cast long shadows into the future,
What future are we going into?

What is the future of humanity in the next century?
The next thousand years,
Is it more shades of what we have seen already?
What has been before,
Enmity,
Conquest and dominance.

Or can we discover something new?
Something as grand as the realisation,
The realisation that we are just a speck,
In the infinity and scope of what it is to exist in the universe,
Can humanity rouse itself to a point where we reflect the infinite magnitude of existence?
In the life and existence, we create on this planet,
How would life look like?
How would this planet look like?
What would life be?
Are we capable of this?

Loss

The pain that comes with it,
Ceaseless,
Endless,
And deep,
When something that was close to you,
A part of you,
Is gone,
Gone forever.

How does one live with it?
Learn to live with it,
Find new meaning,
New purpose,
How do you learn to see through the confusion and pain?
Can you ever?
Or does it just calcify,
Become a lump in your consciousness,
A lump in your soul,
A bump,
A groove,
A callous,
To remind you of what once was,
But alas can never be again.

The pain of reality,
The reality of reality,
That you can love something so much,
Be so close to something,
And you can lose it,
Lose it forever,
The pain like an endless vortex,
A whirlpool of despair and emotion,
The reality of life,
The real reality of it.

Will Africa Ever Catch Up

The vast gap between it and the developed nations,
Politically,
Economically,
Infrastructurally,
Technologically,
Institutionally,
Militarily,
Will Africa ever catch up?

From the deep dark hole of history,
And the problems of the present day,
Will Africa ever catch up?
Will its people ever have an equal footing on the world stage?
Its nations be seen as equal in the eyes of other nations,
Will Africa ever catch up?

Or will it forever be confined to being called the third world,
A place for wealth extraction and exploitation by the powerful nations,
A minnow in the eyes of the powerful.

Will Africa ever catch up?
Will a new class of political leader arise?
Inspired, determined and suffused with good intent,

For she needs this type of leader,
Will the vibrant energy of her people be captured for the good of her?
Their minds harnessed and directed towards transformative change,
For a brighter future for her,
A better future,
Then, what's been before,
Will Africa ever catch up?

Can We Reimagine Politics

Reimagine world governance?
Reimagine economics?
The zero-sum game can't be our highest model,
Where others win,
And others lose,
Nations looking after their own interests,
Companies,
And individuals.

Is this it for humanity?
Is this our highest state?
Our most enlightened state?
Self-interest,
Or can we imagine something better.

The zero-sum game was the way of the past,
Will it be so today?
Tomorrow,
And so on,
Is this the way reality is?
One wins and one loses,
Or can there be another way?

Love

It is that thing that makes life worth it,
Whatever it is that you love,
A person,
A thing,
A past time,
Love makes it all worth it.

Even though life is full of suffering,
Full of pain,
Love seems to be the thing we were given,
In the strangeness of it all,
To make life bearable,
To make life enjoyable,
To provide an antidote to the darkness,
To give us something to hold onto,
Something to be inspired by,
Love.

Imagine

Imagine if we all got along,
Imagine if there was no war,
Never been war,
Imagine if it didn't matter whether you were on the left or right,
Black or white,
Sunni or Shia,
Palestinian or Israeli,
Protestant or Catholic,
And everything else,
Not that it matters what you are,
But that we make it matter,
Often in ways that cause rancour and pain.

Imagine if there was no slavery,
Never had been slavery,
Or colonialism and conquest,
Others profiting from the pain and misery of others,
Their death,
What would that mean about humanity?
What would that say?
How would life look like?
Who would we be?

Imagine if all politicians meant what they said,
Didn't trade in misleading propaganda and slogans,
Didn't inspire division and hatred,
Using things that divide in their quest for power and to have their way,
Not all but some.

Imagine if there was no poverty,
If somehow, we made the world work for everyone,
Not everyone has to be rich,
But if everyone had enough and was okay,
Enough food to eat and a warm safe place to sleep,
That's all one needs.

Imagine if the world was fair,
Or we made it as fair as possible,
Imagine if we strived for this,
All of us,
Imagine,
What would we be?
What would life be?

Yes, life is unfair,
Nature's way is survival of the fittest,
Nature dictates that survival is the name of the game,
But shouldn't being human mean, we overcome that?
Shouldn't that be what it means to be human?
Imagine,
Imagine if it was.

We were given the freedom and the ability to make it so,
Imagine if we had meaningful dialogue,
About all the issues that divide us,
The issues that matter,
Imagine if we solved all our problems,
The quixotic musings of a hopeless dreamer.

Life is Beautiful

It is,
Yes, for the obvious things,
Nature,
Beauty,
Love,
Music,
Joy.

But it's also beautiful,
For the not so obvious things,
The things we go through,
The struggle,
The strife,
The pain,
Teaching us that we are truly alive,
Testing us.

It's beautiful for the brief moments,
The brief moments of clarity,
The brief moments of ecstasy,
Against it all,
Against all that life is,
All that life brings,
All that we face,
Against it all.

Yet here we are,
How beautiful,
The human story,
This tragic tale,
This epic tale,
This awe-inspiring occurrence,
Human life,
Life,
It's beautiful,
For how long will our story be told?

The Belgian Congo

King Leopold,
King of Kings,
You chopped hands,
Took life,
By the millions,
Many millions,
For the rubber,
For the wealth,
Incredible wealth.

Is this the price of opulence?
The price of wealth?
Unimaginable wealth,
The piles of bodies,
And yet life moves on,
Like it never happened,
The victors in the castles,
Living lavishly,
And the victims,
Left to their squalor,
The strange irony of life.

Some speak of justice,
Some speak of karma,

Yet I don't see it,
For victory is absolute,
And so is defeat,
To the winner go the spoils,
And that is the way,
The way it is.

King Leopold,
You chopped hands,
For the rubber,
For the wealth,
The profit motive,
Is this really the height of human enlightenment?
What we base our whole existence around on this planet,
King Leopold,
What a life to live,
For the rubber,
For the wealth.

America, Russia, China

The West, Russia, China
The balance of power in our world,
Vying for superiority,
Vying for dominance,
Vying for supremacy,
The world's superpowers,
Each obsessed by their own interests,
Blinded by ideology,
Blinded by a sense of self,
Seemingly inexorably at odds.

One fears the inevitable,
A hot war as they say,
And the fate of human kind,
Hard to determine in such a scenario,
In this hyper technological era,
The means for war and destruction,
Augmented by human invention,
Even nuclear,
As these super powers posture,
One fears the worst,
One can only fear the worst,
As divisions deepen,
Conflict seems inevitable.

Yet one dares to ask,
What would it take to bridge the gap?
Could these nations ever see eye to eye?
Ever discover real human cooperation,
Or are the differences too deep?
The divisions too entrenched,
The need for dominance too strong,
The desire for supremacy too alluring,
The instinct for self-preservation unshakeable and the politics too layered with distrust.

Perhaps to even ask,
Is too pollyannaish,
Human nature is too incontrovertible,
War and enmity are in our nature,
Mutually assured destruction,
The only possible outcome,
The only question left to ask then,
Is how long do we have left?

Human Cooperation

Human unity,
Human understanding,
Is it possible?
Is it within the scope of human capability?

A thriving Africa,
A thriving Asia,
A thriving Europe,
A thriving Americas,
A thriving world,
Or are we destined to see the world through a competitive lens?

Success seen and determined by the failure of others,
The domination over others,
Or can we harness the meaningful aspects of competition,
The meaningful aspects of cooperation,
Why should one have to lose for another to win?
In the most meaningful sense,
In the most meaningful sense,
It after all is one planet,
One human race.

Yes, life has realities,
Life must be survived,
Success must be earned,
Work must be done,
This is true,
This is real,
And it is good,
It gives life meaning.

In a race someone must come first,
The rest lose,
This is true,
But in the grandest sense of life,
Why can't we all win?
In the most meaningful sense,
In the most meaningful sense,
After all,
It's only one planet.

Humanity

Killing,
Spilling,
Blood,
Ending life,
Taking life,
The human condition,
Seems so strange to a poet,
Why it must be this way,
Why we are this way.

It's clear to see,
In the poet's mind,
That there is only one human race on this planet,
This rock floating through space,
Floating in space,
Our only home,
Why can't we share it?
In peace,
Why is it beyond us?

Are we thusly limited?
To think in such limited ways,
Race,
Ethnicity,

Nationality,
Borders,
Them and Us,
Superiority and inferiority,
Better than.

It seems strange to a poet,
It seems strange to a peace-loving man,
Killing,
Spilling blood,
Hatred,
Geopolitics,
It seems strange to a poet,
It seems strange to a peace-loving man.

Race

The human race,
The great frontier,
The final frontier,
A toxic history,
A brutal history,
A toxic reality,
A brutal reality,
Race as a source of difference,
Race as a source of division,
Race as a source of hatred.

How do we put the human in human race?
This is the great question,
For all we might achieve,
For all the technology we might create,
Even if we learn all the secrets of the Universe,
Learn to traverse the Universe,
We have achieved nothing,
If we don't conquer this final frontier,
We will just export our disharmony to the wide expanse of space.

It seems to me,
Before we conquer space,
We must conquer the disunity of humanity,
Surely that would be our greatest achievement,
And truly everything would be possible then.

Race,
The human race,
Our final frontier,
Our greatest frontier,
How can our shared existence reflect the greatest aspect of being a human race?

One Chance it Seems

One chance to be you,
One chance to live,
Live as you,
One chance to be,
One life,
One opportunity,
This life,
Your life,
This one life.

Ostensibly this is true,
You certainly get one chance to be you,
Even if you come back again,
As some schools of thought teach,
It is true though to say,
To be this version of you,
In this life,
In each life perhaps,
It's only one chance,
Just as we have one planet,
We have one chance,
One chance to get it right.

Through all life's complications,
Through all life's challenges,
We get one chance,
We have one planet,
One home,
One life.

Amazing beyond imagination,
To be,
A miracle of all miracles,
Each breath,
A manifestation of the grandeur of the universe,
The grandeur and miracle of occurrence.

To be,
To be,
One life,
One opportunity,
Life,
Can it be everything it could be?

Racism

Malice and ignorance,
Open hatred,
A wicked invention,
A wicked inheritance,
Reducing the value of human life,
Reducing the value of what it is to be human.

Will we ever get past this reality?
Will we ever get past this inheritance?
Will we ever transcend it?
Transcend it into a new reality,
Or are its teachings too entrenched?
Its divisions too deep,
The belief too powerful,
Too enticing,
The prejudice too hard to overcome.

Once taught,
To unteach seems impossible,
Once the beliefs are held,
Adherence to them becomes a matter of life and death,
What can be done about such conditioning?
Which can infect so powerfully,
So deeply,

So convincingly,
Will there ever be a day we rid the world of racism?
What a day it would be.

Human History

The human story,
A trail of bloodshed from the earliest times,
The road to modernity is laden with bloodshed,
And to this day we shed blood,
This is humanity,
This is life,
Our story.

At times we point fingers,
And look for perpetrators,
But the only truth,
Is that bloodshed is the human story,
And we are all capable,
Only question is,
Is that our whole story?
And is that how it's always going to be?

To Look Up

To look up at the sky,
To see the stars at night,
A glimpse into the great beyond,
Each and every one of those stars,
A glimpse into infinity,
A glimpse into eternity,
The beyond of the beyond.

A reality beyond what the eye can see,
A reality beyond what our telescopes can see,
A reality beyond what our greatest minds can imagine and decipher,
Yet we are here,
Small, limited and bound,
Everything we are,
The good and the bad,
What a juxtaposition.

Infinity against the finitude of humanity,
Our state of affairs,
Perhaps a fitting reflection of our limitation,
Small and bound,
And we do act as such,
In so many ways,

When all one has to do is look up,
Look up and see,
A glimpse into infinity,
A glimpse into eternity,
A glimpse into the realisation,
That reality is greater,
Greater than our limitations.

Oh, The Potential

The infinite potential of humanity,
If we saw what was possible,
If we captured the possibility of possibility,
What could be possible?
If we put down the guns,
Abandoned the isms,
Saw a greater vision,
The greatest vision of what is possible,
And we had the will to work for it.

Oh, the potential,
The infinite potential,
Of what we are capable of,
From antiquity,
The great structures, wisdom and knowledge of the past,
To what's possible today,
The very new, rapidly and ever evolving technological world,
If we harnessed all our potential,
For the greatest possibility,
The greatest possibility of humanity,
What would be possible?

Even in the Fog of War

The danger of war,
At risk of loss of life and limb,
When you would have thought all lives should matter,
You are reminded that they don't,
Your black skin still marks you,
Your dark skin still marks you,
How is it in the so-called civilised lands,
The value of all human beings is not yet established?

How can you on one hand claim to be enlightened and civilised,
Yet on the other hand you fail to see the full value of another,
Where is the enlightenment?
Where is the civilisation?
Even in the fog of war,
As all flee to save their very precious lives,
You are still only black,
Not worth saving,
You don't belong,
Less than.

Life Observed

Life in all forms,
Life at all levels,
This strange crucible,
This strange mix of highs and lows,
This strange thing,
The human being,
Human existence,
So complex.

Beguiling,
Bewildering,
Enchanting,
Visceral,
But ultimately strange,
So strange,
What we are,
What it is,
Life,
Inscrutable,
For all its wonder and confusion.

The More Things Change

The more they stay the same,
So the saying goes,
It seems the same perils that have plagued humanity in the past,
Still plague humanity today,
And will most like plague humanity in the future,
Maybe it's foolish to think it could ever be different,
Human nature is entrenched and unchanging.

We must kill,
We must hate,
We must lie, deceive and manipulate,
We must dominate,
We must fear,
We must shun,
We must judge,
Even as we err ourselves,
To err is to be human,
That is the epitome of humanity itself.

To imagine a world without discord,
To imagine a world without disunity,
To imagine a world without injustice,
Is to imagine a world without humanity,

Maybe enlightenment is found in accepting this,
And living with this reality,
After all, we all perish,
The suffering comes to an end for all,
Living comes to an end for all.

So, what is, is,
What will be will be,
So, when the cold harshness of reality stings,
Perhaps one must accept,
That it is as it should be,
The whys and wherefores,
Well,
That's for entities much greater and wiser than us,
Much wiser than we are.

And perhaps it is in surrendering to a greater reality,
That one might find peace,
So, when hate shows itself,
Human discord,
War and destruction,
Suffering, killing,
Know that it is as it should be,
For it has been that way since humanity has been aware of itself.

It is that way now,
And it most likely will be that way in the future,
It is maybe for whatever God or coincidence of creation responsible for our apparition to know why it must be this way.

Humanity

The manifold faces,
The manifold faces that have come and gone,
The lives lived,
The lives to be lived,
A vast ocean of souls,
An endless stream of these organic beings,
Throughout time,
An incredible thought.

Even more so to contemplate what it all means,
What it's all for,
So much that we share,
In this truly miraculous thing we call life,
The many faces,
A vast sea of faces that have come and gone,
Stretching through time,
Our time on this planet,
To truly contemplate the purpose,
What it all means,
In light of all life is.

The light and the dark,
The triumph and the trials,
So much history,

So many wars,
The multitude of endless wars,
So much killing,
So much killing,
The laughter,
The friendships,
The sheer madness of life,
The sheer madness of actually being alive.

The magnitude of the combined miracles that make life possible,
The sheer glory of it,
The grandeur of it,
If only we could harness the greatest essence of it,
The greatest essence of being alive,
Capture it,
Observe it,
Learn from it,
So that the sheer prodigiousness of being alive,
The sheer stupendousness of it,
Is never lost on us ever again,
And we can harness that truth,
Harness it for humanity,
Harness it forever,
If only.

How to Bridge the Gap

The gap between infinity and humanity,
The gap between eternity and humanity,
The gap between all that is,
And all that we are,
The gap between the all-redemptive power of true love,
And the all-consuming power of hate and division.

How to bridge the gap between the wonder of our place in the Universe,
And our location and seeming isolation here on this planet,
The gap between the greatness that could be,
And the reality of the existence that is,
The gap between limitation and all that could be truly possible.

Our sun is just one star,
The closest star to us in a galaxy with hundreds of billions of other stars,
In a universe with billions of galaxies,
A universe that is said to be endless and ever expanding,
And who knows how it first came into existence,
Or it has always been,
These truly monumental imponderables,
Where all we can do is postulate.

And how this magnificent grandeur,
Seems to escape us every day,
As we struggle and toil,
As we see to being human,
In all its varied ways.

Unimaginable greatness and meaning,
And unimaginable meaninglessness,
Side by side,
How to bridge the gap,
The gap between the endless scope of the Universe,
possibility and all that is,
And us,
Finite contradictory beings.

Flags

Flags and nations,
So much done in the name of flags,
So much done in the name of nations,
So much significance we put on the flags,
So much significance we put on the nations,
Base so much of our identity on the flags, on the nations we identify with.

Some will kill and die for their flags and nations,
Pledge allegiance,
Swear allegiance,
In some nations its compulsory,
Mandatory.

A nation,
A creation,
A flag,
A creation,
Artificial,
Yet there is nothing artificial about the depth of feeling that wells up in those passionate about their flags,
In those passionate about their nations,
We believe our nation should come first,
Only our compatriots matter,

We should promote the interests of our nation's first,
At the grandest appreciation of what humanity is,
What life is,
It seems a strange contrivance.

This obsession and allegiance to flags and nations,
At the grandest level of observation, it's nonsensical,
Asinine,
But at the level of diminished and everyday insight,
It makes perfect sense,
To kill for our flags and nations,
To hate in the name of our flags and nations,
To hoard all the resources of the world in the name of our flags,
In the name of our nations.

And it matters not the cost to those who wave other flags,
And live in other nations,
Live elsewhere,
What a strange state of affairs,
At the highest level of appreciation,
At the highest appreciation of what life is,
What a strange state of affairs.

Perhaps it's Time

Time to really think about what it means to be a human being,
Time to really discuss what it means to be a human being,
What it means to be a collective on this planet we call home,
The apex predator,
The most influential living being on this planet,
The most consequential,
For the planet and for us, humans.

Perhaps it's time to discuss,
Really discuss where humanity is going,
Where we see ourselves in the next thousand years,
What our future is,
Our shared future,
How we share this home,
How we share this planet,
We have bungled through,
Muddled our way through somehow from antiquity to modernity.

We have somehow found our way,
From disparate warring groups spread across the globe,
Separated by distance and geography,
And we discovered each other,
As time went by.

Conquered and pillaged,
As technology shrunk the world,
To this day we live in of rapid global travel and telecommunication,
A brave new world,
It's a very new world,
Not too long been birthed,
How do we traverse it together and better than we have up until now?

The whole world is connected now,
What does this mean for the future?
What can we make it mean?
We have muddled our way into the twenty first century,
By some miracle we haven't killed ourselves off along the way,
Though we have tried,
And how we have tried,
Yet we are still here,
However, instead of muddling and bungling our way to modernity as we have,
In this modernity, maybe we can take control.

Yes, let's take control,
Let's wrest the narrative from fate, chance and prejudice,
Let's plot our path,
Like intrepid, inspired visionaries,
Let's be intentional,
Let's be wilful,
Let's be deliberate,
Let's be inspired,

Inspired by the greatest vision of ourselves,
We have all the tools to create a paradise,
The economics,
The farming,
The technology,
The science,
The lessons from history,
And the wisdom and enlightenment of all the greatest minds that have come before.

We truly have no excuse,
But for a lack of vision,
A lack of imagination,
A lack of inspiration,
A lack of direction.

The Collective History of Humanity

The many cultures,
The many languages,
Beliefs and traditions.

Humanity,
Teeming with diversity,
A kaleidoscope betraying the complexity of humanity,
A rich tapestry,
The human story,
The collective beauty of it all.

How do we capture this?
Capture the best aspects of ourselves,
Against all that is dark and unsavoury,
Seemingly impossible to escape,
It can consume you,
Yet one can only dream,
Dream the dreamer's dream,
Dream of a brighter vision of humanity.

After all,
That's what dreams are for,
A means to escape from the drudgery and the mundanity,

So, a poet can only dream,
Dream the impossible dream,
Dream it could be possible,
Wish it could be possible,
To capture the greatest qualities of humanity,
And dream of something better,
Something greater.

Apparently, We are Presided Over by a Loving God

So, the religions say,
A loving, benevolent and kind God,
Yet in life sometimes,
A lot of the time,
It can be hard to see this love, kindness and benevolence,
In all the evils of this world,
The wars,
The brutal dictators,
Injustice and disease.

The brutal demands of survival,
Which mean flesh must consume flesh to survive,
In the animal kingdom,
And we too are part of that system,
The brutality of one living creature having to kill and consume another to survive,
The sheer insanity of the reality of this,
The asymmetry of the world,
Dominion of the conquerors over the conquered,
The consumption of life through power and brutality.

One can wonder,
Where is this loving God?

Where is this kind God?
Where is this benevolent God?
What loving God would contrive and preside over such a reality?
The list of horrors of life are endless,
Pain, suffering and cruelty are real things,
So, one can truly wonder,
Where is this God?
Where is this loving God?

In all the disastrous fates, tragedies and circumstances that can befall one,
Where is this God?
A thought then,
Maybe God lets life be,
God lets us be,
Let's all that can happen,
Happen.

At the highest extent of freedom,
Maybe God lets us be free to be,
In every way,
Let's life be all it can be in every way that it can be,
And that way, anything can happen,
Both good and bad.

But it's good to observe,
That good and bad is our meaning,
Good and bad is our meaning as human beings,
Perhaps too that's why it can be relative,
Perhaps where there is no humanity,

And devoid of human perception and reason,
There is no meaning,
No good and bad,
Just occurrence,
Occurrence and being.

And maybe it's at this level,
That the true beauty of it all exists,
Just the happenstance of occurrence,
Devoid of meaning,
Just the possibility,
The possibility of everything that can happen,
Happening.

Maybe there's some solace there,
Some inspiration,
That we are truly let to be,
Free to be,
To the fullest extent,
To the absolute extent of freedom,
Free to be all things,
All that happens,
All that is,
Allows us to be,
In every way possible.

And perhaps there is a challenge there for humanity,
A rallying cry,
That we are free to be,
Free to choose our destiny,
So, what will we choose?

More of the same,
More of what's already been,
Or something greater,
What will we be?
Humanity can choose,
Has the power to choose,
The power to create,
What a blessing bestowed.

To be Black

Is to have the worst assumed about you,
To be economically dislocated,
As a vestige of history,
To be black,
Is to be geographically dislocated,
To be an immigrant,
Not an expat.

To be black is to have your continent,
Your place of origin, your home be in a state of disrepair,
As the echoes of the exploits of past and present reverberate
from the past into the present,
To be black,
Is to be at the bottom of the human social ladder,
To have been placed there deliberately by the architects of
empire,
The architects of racial subjugation.

To be black,
Is to be looked down upon,
You can't lead,
You can't be at a high station,
To be black,

Is to be clawing yourself out from the ignominy of history and a diminished social standing with every breath you take,
To be black,
Is to inherit a tragic story,
To be part of a collective trauma,
To be told you are intellectually inferior,
If not just inferior.

To be black is to have others believe this,
Believe it passionately,
Believe it as though their lives depended on it,
And build edifices around this belief,
To be black is to endure,
To endure and endure.

I long for the day this stops to be true,
I long for the day being black just means being black,
I long for a transformation in the story of being black,
In the condition of being black,
I long for an end to the ailments afflicting the black race,
I long for an end to the ailments afflicting us all,
I long for the day I can go anywhere on this planet and not have my blackness follow me,
I long for the day only my humanity follows me.

As the overarching shadow of history casts its shade over the modern day,
I long for the day we can leave the worst elements of history behind,
And only bring forward the best,
I long for the day when your heritage is just your heritage,
And we can marvel together at our shared heritage.

They had to say black is beautiful because others believed it wasn't,
They had to say black lives matter because others thought they did not,
I long for the day we see the beauty and the value in all that is.

The Happenstance of our Existence

A marvellous occurrence,
Some believe it's by the hand of some deity,
Others who shun the idea of a God believe there was just some big bang,
Whatever you believe about the modality of our actuality,
What is clear is we are here,
For this there is no confusion,
Our actuality is a reality.

This alone should inspire enough wonder,
This alone should inspire some kind of sense of a great commonality that we all share,
At least I think so,
To think we might not exist,
But we do,
It makes everything pale in comparison.

Surely,
The tribalism,
The racism,
The xenophobia,
The hatred,
Surely it pales in comparison,

Dwarfed by the miracle that we all exist,
When we might not have existed,
At least I think so.

We exist together,
On this solitary planet,
Surely there is more than enough there to create some kind of solidarity,
Enough to make the warring look foolish,
The greed,
The corruption,
The abuse of power.

At least I think so,
At least I think so,
Whatever the deity,
Whatever the modality by which we have come to exist,
We do exist,
Together,
Surely this must be able to inspire something truly amazing about us,
What we share,
What we owe each other.

Something much greater than what we have been able to create and envisage so far,
At least I think so,
At least I think so.

The Sun is Always Set to Rise

So don't let your hope set on you,
Even under the darkest clouds,
And the most tempestuous weather,
The sun is always there, shining behind the clouds,
Even during the darkest, deepest night,
And it's impossible to see your way in the darkness,
Even then,
When it's time,
Day will break and the sun will rise.

So, even when it seems there is no hope,
The darkness will come to pass,
In time,
For the sun always rises,
It always has and it always will,
As long as the universe remains the same,
The sun will always rise,
So, for this,
There is always hope for you,
Hope for humanity.

That even when you lose your way,
When we lose our way,

We will somehow always find our way back onto the right path,
For the sun always rises,
Yes, it does,
So, always look to hope,
Don't ever let your hope set on you,
For the sun always rises.

Our Attachment

To something so temporary,
So ephemeral,
Transient and finite,
Something so finite as life,
It seems neurotic,
A strange neurosis,
Maybe a neurosis that explains the strangeness of our behaviour.

We value our lives,
Our own lives so much,
That often it supersedes the lives of others,
This explains so much,
Our attachment to our own lives,
As individuals,
As groups,
The desire to survive,
Blinding.

Something so ephemeral,
So transient,
Maybe if we were not so attached,
To our own lives,
Our own survival,

The survival of the groups we identify with,
Maybe we might be more at ease,
More at peace,
After all your very brief moment here,
Will come to pass,
It comes to pass for all of us.

Maybe in accepting this,
There's an answer there somewhere,
Maybe we might not be so neurotic,
Neurotic about preserving our own lives,
At the expense of others.

As one wrecks the mind,
Looking for solutions for peace,
Antidotes for human discord,
One can only hypothesise,
Postulate,
Search the consciousness,
Search the ether,
Search the ether for answers.

Maybe it's Possible

Maybe it's possible,
Humanity doesn't sprint towards transformation,
Humanity doesn't sprint towards change,
It progresses inch by painful inch towards a better day,
For not too long-ago blacks hung from trees,
Their bodies mutilated,
To raucous jeering and celebrating mobs of whites in the land of the free,
To die and have no justice,
As though that precious life mattered for absolutely nothing,
As the perpetrators carried on with their lives,
Free to raise their offspring,
With impunity and freedom,
Protected by the law.

Yet inch by painful inch blacks won their rights,
Won their freedoms all over the world,
Delivered from apartheid,
Delivered from colonialism,
Delivered from slavery,
And yes, are freer today than they were just a not too distant yesterday ago,
Inch by painful inch,

Like the wild forest fire that burns all in an intense heat,
But in the process lays the ground for new shoots,
A new forest,
New life,
We progress through the blazing inferno of injustice,
The blazing inferno of war,
The blazing inferno of terrible hatred,
Inch by painful inch towards a better day.

Maybe this is the way,
This is the only way it is for us, humans,
To bring forth something new and beautiful,
Through the scalding embers of tragedy, pain and trial,
Inch by inch,
Inch by painful inch towards a better day.

Maybe it's possible,
Maybe it's possible there will be one great day,
A day of unbridled joy, peace and tranquillity,
Even if it's just for one day,
Inch by painful inch.

Why is the Sky Blue

Gases and particles in the earth's atmosphere,
Scatter sunlight in all directions,
Blue light is scattered more than other colours,
Because it travels as shorter, smaller waves,
This is why the sky is blue,
One of the many miracles of existence,
That allows us to look up and see the sky we have come to know.

There is a real mystery about life,
A real and truly majestic mystery,
A deep and wondrous mystery,
The unquantifiable numbers of miracles that constitute all that is,
That make life what it is,
That make life happen,
Some miracles that we will never know,
Existence beyond our purview,
Life beyond what we can sense, perceive and even imagine,
It exists,
And it's out there.

We are part of a truly great universal wonder,
Yet we are also humans,

In every way that we are humans,
That which is truly great,
And all that which is deplorable,
All happening concomitantly,
Even in the individual,
And the greater body of humanity.

We have been endowed with a gift,
The gift to be animate and capable of so much,
All that we have managed to do and create,
And in such a short space of time we are even looking to conquer space,
Yet, we are also humans,
It's the greatest dichotomy,
The great duality.

So, it leads this poet to wonder,
It leads this poet to ask,
What is really possible for humanity?
Can we create peace on earth?
Is utopia a possibility or a delusion?
For this poet utopia doesn't mean some nirvanic realm where everything is perfect,
It means us making life work as well for all as much as we possibly can.

The realities of life are not lost on this poet,
The many challenges and competing priorities of life,
It's not about hopeless idealism and romanticism,
Such romanticism and idealism can be dangerous and lead to carnage.

For this poet, utopia means pragmatism and idealism coexisting,
But mostly for this poet, utopia means no more war,
For this poet utopia means the possibility of imagining five, ten, a hundred or more years where not a single human life is lost because of war,
For this poet, utopia means imagining this could be possible,
For this poet, utopia means imagining if we could just build and not destroy.

For this poet, utopia also means no more racism,
No more tribalism or xenophobia,
For this poet utopia means fairer systems of governance and resource distribution,
No more political violence and repression,
If not violence in general,
For this poet, utopia means working together,
Surely, we can manage that,
For this poet, this seems to be within the realm of human possibility,
This seems to be within our purview,
Why is the sky blue this poet asks?
Because life is beautiful.

If you have reached this far, I would like to say, thank you for reading my book to the end. I hope you have enjoyed my assortment of poems and my meditations on life. I hope the poems have spoken to you, touched you and also been enjoyable or captivating.

I find life intriguing, fascinating, and I think a lot about it if not every day. The meaning and purpose of life in light of how challenging it can be and always hope that the world can be a better place for all. Generally, I feel humanity has made great strides to this end and perhaps we just need some finishing touches.

I believe that there is absolutely no reason why the world cannot be an amazing place for everyone, and in many ways, it is, we just need to work on certain aspects where we let ourselves down as a species and this is what I hope I inspired with some of my poems. A vision of a fantastic world. Why not.

In conclusion, I would like to say that this book is a triumph of light over darkness. Coming to the end of 2016 in November, I went to a ten-day silent meditation retreat at the recommendation of a friend. I went not really knowing what I was walking into but just led by curiosity and a burning desire to discover a deeper meaning to life.

During the retreat, I ended up having a deeply mystical experience which was reality and perspective shifting. However, life got dark after the retreat because I suffered what is medically known as a psychotic episode, and found myself in a psychiatric hospital for a month. Upon release I got into a deeper and darker depression and anxiety.

My daughter was born as I was coming out of that period of deep depression and anxiety which lasted over two years. Unfortunately for me, that was not the end of my troubles. Subsequent relapses led to the end of my marriage, and the covid pandemic led to a failed business venture and financial ruin.

Dealing with all this heart break, how life could be so cruel, this book came out. A real triumph over darkness. I almost gave it all up, but this book stands as hope for the greatness of what is possible in life – overcoming insurmountable obstacles and hope for the future.

We all have personal challenges, and I hope everyone can overcome their personal challenges and we all can overcome our collective challenges as a species.

I say to the reader, no matter what you are going through, no matter what you will ever go through, never give up.

I named the book after my daughter because she is beautiful and ultimately life is beautiful too and I want her to have a beautiful life and the world to be a beautiful place for her. She was the light at the end of my dark tunnel.

As it turns out, this book is also written and concluded at a time when Russia has invaded Ukraine and the use of nuclear weapons has raised its head as a real possibility in an all-out war. There is a real possibility of a global apocalypse as incredible and unbelievable as that sounds.

Putting Putin's postulations and the West's perceived moral outrage into perspective, this war epitomises everything that inspired me to write my poetry. The sheer complexity of human beings, human life and the human condition.

The smoke and mirrors of politicians, geopolitics and self-interest as each side hides their own nefarious actions past and present whilst pointing the finger at the other. How very human all that is. Furthermore, the sight of black and brown people being refused entry and sanctuary in some of the neighbouring European countries everyone was fleeing to from Ukraine and the racist treatment of black and brown people by some of the Ukrainians themselves. Coupled with the reactions and commentary of some of the professional European journalists who were mortified and aghast that a war of this nature could be happening in Europe, to blonde hair, blue-eyed Europeans and not in some third world developing country where presumably it is okay for such things to happen, it is okay for those people to die. As if ignorant of the history of war in Europe and seemingly having an apparent hierarchy on the value of life. How very human all that is too.

It is into this reality that I write, the reality of life in all its ways as I look for the beauty of life, the beauty in all of it as strange as that may sound. The hope being that, if we can discover the beauty in all of life, we might be able to create a beautiful life here on this planet. Failing that, it is hard to see how much hope humanity has in light of all the challenges we face.

Economically with wealth distribution and economic justice. The asymmetric history and reality of the world. The climate emergency as some claim we are at the brink of catastrophe. War in a hyper technological nuclear age and the culture and identity wars. Racism and political ideological warfare.

This is the human condition.

I really hope my poetry has spoken to this. Portrayed a deeper contemplation of life and a deeper appreciation of life. I also hope my poetry can inspire something positive. I hope my poetry can inspire the reader and hopefully inspire me too.

However, ultimately, I hope I can be at peace because I have told the Universe how I feel and I hope you can find peace in your life too. I hope everyone can find peace.

And one more for the road,

Like Raindrops

All birthed from the same clouds right up on high,
Due to fall inexorably towards the ground,
Subject to the vagaries and capricious nature of the elements,
The winds of life,
Our lives and experiences,
As individual as the billions of raindrops falling from the sky,
All destined to meet the end,
The inevitable dissolution of that solitary raindrop,
As it meets the ground and is consumed by the earth,
Into eternity,
The eternal change of form and state,
Into something else,
Something beyond what the naked eye can see,
Life's journey,
Like the raindrop.

To exist only for the briefest moment,
The beginning and the end,
After that,
Gone forever,
With only the mark it makes on the ground left as a memory,
And that too,
To be wiped away by time and the shifting sands,
That is life,

This brief moment we have,
This brief moment to be,
Like raindrops we are,
Beautiful tiny manifold raindrops.